EXCELLENCE

in

Ministry

D0701935

BRIAN BRODERSEN

Excellence in Ministry

Copyright © 2008 by Brian Brodersen

Published by Calvary Chapel Publishing (CCP),
a resource ministry of Calvary Chapel of Costa Mesa
3800 South Fairview Road
Santa Ana, CA 92704

First printing, 2008

All Scripture quotations, unless otherwise indicated, are taken from the New King James Version®. Copyright © 1982 by Thomas Nelson, Inc. Used by permission. All rights reserved.

Scriptures marked KJV are taken from the King James Version of the Bible.

Cover layout and design by Doug Long

Editing and internal layout by Romy Godding

ISBN: 978-1-59751-043-1

Printed in the United States of America

PREFACE

I believe that the primary objective of the Great Commission, which is to make disciples of all nations, is best accomplished through the establishing of local churches. The local church is the place where people who want to know, love, and serve God are helped to do so. We who are in the ministry ought to endeavor to do church in a way that brings glory to God and helps as many people as possible to become disciples of Jesus Christ.

If there is confusion in our minds about our calling or about the task, if we are ill equipped for the job or perhaps lacking in practical wisdom, we can end up hindering rather than helping those who are seeking to grow in their relationship with Jesus.

I've written this book for those who are just starting out in the ministry and for those who are thinking about giving up. For those who are just getting started, I hope this book will help you avoid some of the mistakes that I and others have made that have hindered rather than helped the progress of the church. For those who are discouraged and considering giving up, my hope is that you will be encouraged to stay the course and make the necessary adjustments that will lead to a joyful and fruitful ministry experience.

Brian Brodersen
January 2008

CONTENTS

chapter 1

THE CALL TO MINISTRY

For every high priest taken from among men is appointed for men in things pertaining to God ... And no man takes this honor to himself, but he who is called by God.

—Hebrews 5:1, 4

To be a minister of God's Word is, in my opinion, the greatest privilege a man could ever enjoy. But along with that privilege comes a great responsibility; therefore, this ministry should never be approached lightly nor should any man take it upon himself. A quote from Charles Spurgeon makes the point succinctly: "He that should take upon himself to be a policeman, and go and do the work of arresting others, without having received a commission, must be in danger of being [arrested] himself, for being a deceiver. [Therefore] if I had not been called to the ministry, and had no seal of it, I had better leave it alone, lest I go without God's commission."[1] Those who minister the Word of God must be called by God to do so. The question is then: How can a man know whether or not he is called? Let me give you seven indicators to look for that I believe suggest the call of God on a man's life.

Desire

There will be an intense, all-absorbing desire for the work. The man God calls into the ministry is overcome by the conviction that he can do nothing else. He finds himself restless at what he was previously quite content doing. A passion for Christ and His work begins to overtake him. He feels compelled to expend more and more of his time and energy on the things of the kingdom. The man who is called gives himself for service and yields himself up to any act of service, no matter how small or great. Whether it be sharing the gospel with an unbeliever, encouraging a fellow Christian, attending a prayer meeting, helping set up for the worship service, or cleaning up afterward, he does it all with zeal and joy.

I heard Greg Laurie tell the story of his first great ministry opportunity. He was to purchase a part needed to repair one of the doors of the church. He approached this occasion for service with all the zeal of a man sent on a great mission by God. The zeal with which he went about such a mundane task is the kind of thing evidenced in those who are called to the ministry.

Spiritual Understanding

There will be an understanding of the Scriptures, along with a desire to share them with others. Pastoral ministry is primarily about sharing the Word of God. Jesus said to Peter, "Feed My sheep."[2] When Peter wrote to the early church leaders, he said, "Shepherd the flock of God which is among you."[3] Paul instructed Timothy to give attention to reading, to exhortation, and to doctrine.[4] Therefore, those who are called to the ministry are going to have an understanding of the Scriptures that is above and beyond that of the average Christian. There will also be a burning desire to share the Word with others.

Gifting

There will be a God-given ability to teach. How can a person know whether they are gifted to teach? The answer is quite simple: if there are people who learn from you, then you are able to teach. If you are one of those people who love to give Bible studies and yet no one else seems to be interested, then perhaps God has some other type of ministry for you. Those who are called are apt to teach, which practically means, people will be apt to listen and learn.

Love

The man who is called into the ministry will have a love for God and for people. A love for God would seem to go without saying. But in the long history of the church, there have been many men in ministry who have loved the position, the power, and the prestige far more than they ever loved God; and that problem is not limited to the past. The man who is called to the ministry will not only have a love for God, he will also have a love for people. The ministry is mainly about people, so if a man dislikes his fellow man, the ministry is not the place for him. Jesus loves people, and those who minister in His name must love people as well. I'm not talking about a gushy sentimentalism, but rather a love like that seen in our Lord Jesus—a love that is willing to sacrifice for others, is patient

Jesus loves people, and those who minister in His name must love people as well.

with the weaknesses of others, and that longs to see God's best worked out in the lives of others. I have found over the years that sometimes the smallest act of love can bring the reality of Christ to someone when nothing else could. A smile, a kind word, or just a listening ear goes a long way to communicate the love of Christ.

Humility

The man who is called will have a sense of his own inadequacy. When considering the responsibilities of the minister of the gospel, the apostle Paul said, "And who is sufficient for these things?"[5] Because of the influence of pop psychology on the church, those who are assertive and overflowing with self-confidence are often the first choices for leadership in the church today. In my opinion, no man is ready for the ministry until he can affirm the words of Jesus, "Without Me you can do nothing."[6] Martyn Lloyd-Jones was undoubtedly one of the greatest preachers of the twentieth century. Yet when asked what he personally thought of his own preaching, he said that he wouldn't cross the street to hear himself preach. In that statement, he was simply expressing that underlying sense of weakness and inability that every man truly called of God knows so well.

In my own experience, I find that the longer I serve the Lord, the more obvious my own insufficiencies become. As the years roll by, I find myself despairing more and more of my own abilities and clinging to Jesus for even the smallest task. In almost thirty years of ministry, I have stood before people literally thousands of times to teach God's Word, and yet I am just as dependent on His help today as I was in the beginning. Actually, in many ways, I am even more dependent now because I know experientially that "in me (that is, in my flesh) nothing good dwells."[7] To sum it up, if you marvel at the possibility of God using you, if you stand utterly amazed at the thought of God choosing you for some task, whether great or small, then it is quite probable that God is indeed calling you.

No man is ready for the ministry until he can affirm the words of Jesus, "Without Me you can do nothing."

Holiness

There will be a desire for holiness. The word holiness implies separation from sin and consecration to God. A man who has little concern for holiness is simply not called to the ministry. He might be pursuing the ministry, he might even be in the ministry, but he's not called to the ministry. Paul tells us, "[God] has saved us and called us with a holy calling."[8] If that is true for Christians in general, how much more for ministers of the gospel?

Unholy ministers have been the bane of the church down through the ages and are still one of the primary causes of the church's weakened testimony to the world. God's standard has not changed; the command to "be holy, for I am holy"[9] is as true today as when God originally gave it. Robert Murray M'Cheyne stated it best when he said: "My people's greatest need is my personal holiness."

A man who has little concern for holiness is simply not called to the ministry.

Affirmation from the Church

The church will affirm the call. The body of Christ will acknowledge your gifts by receiving from you. You won't have to try to convince others you're called; they themselves will affirm that by submitting to your leadership. Also, those who are in positions of leadership in the church will affirm the call. After the conversion of Saul of Tarsus, Barnabas, a key leader in the church in Jerusalem, recognized the call of God upon Saul and brought him to the attention of the church.[10] We can expect similar things as a way of confirming our call.

There are, no doubt, many other evidences that we might look for in seeking confirmation of God's call upon our lives; but these are some of the most common indicators that those called into the ministry have experienced.

chapter 2

SHEPHERDING THE FLOCK OF GOD

He will feed His flock like a shepherd; He will gather the lambs with His arm, and carry them in His bosom, and gently lead those who are with young.

—Isaiah 40:11

The above verse is, of course, a prophecy of the ministry of Jesus, but I think it is more than that. It is also a beautiful picture of pastoral ministry.

Pastoral ministry has always been a matter close to the heart of God. Through the prophets Jeremiah and Ezekiel, we hear the Lord thundering judgment against the shepherds who feed themselves and abuse or neglect His flock.[11]

When we come to the New Testament, we find the apostles renouncing those who were peddling the Word of God and exploiting His people. Some of the strongest language in all of Scripture is used to warn false shepherds of the certain judgment that will fall upon those who fleece, rather than feed, the flock of God.[12]

Since God Himself expresses such concern over the care given to His flock, we need to approach the subject with a certain amount of fear and trembling.

What is involved in pastoral ministry? According to the opening verse, pastoral ministry involves three things: feeding, tending, and leading God's people.

Feeding the Flock

Through Jeremiah, the Lord said, "I will set up shepherds over them who shall feed them ..."[13]

The pastor's first responsibility is to feed the flock by faithfully teaching God's Word to them. Bible teaching is perhaps the greatest need in the church today. In the modern church, the appalling ignorance of the Scriptures is largely due to the failure of pastors and leaders to teach the Bible. In many churches, the pulpit is no longer the place where the Word of God is exposited; instead, it is the place where the pastor expresses his opinions about culture, politics, the environment, the latest psychological theory, or perhaps (if the pastor is really hip) the spiritual significance of a popular song, movie, or television program. All of this has left the flock in a weak, sickly, and vulnerable state.

A pastor is to feed the flock; he will answer to God for whether or not he has been faithful to fulfill his responsibility.

Paul said to the Ephesian elders, "For I have not shunned to declare to you the whole counsel of God."[14] That, I believe, is an excellent way of describing what it means to feed the flock. We have the entire Bible, and we should teach all of it—thought by thought, verse by verse, chapter by chapter! Never succumb to the idea that Bible teaching and preaching were all right for past generations, but post-moderns need something special. We are *called* to teach and preach the Word. We don't do it because it's an acceptable method of communication, but because it's God's method declared in His Word!

Bible teaching is perhaps the greatest need in the church today.

Paul said to Timothy: "give attention to reading, to exhortation, to doctrine."[15] He also exhorted him to, "preach the word!"[16] The book of Acts tells us, "They did not cease teaching and preaching Jesus as the Christ."[17]

Growing up spiritually in Calvary Chapel, I have seen this so beautifully exemplified week after week, month after month, year after year. If you're looking for a model to follow, look no further! Don't go running off to this seminar and that conference, searching for the newest gimmick that will help your church grow. Church growth is not our business, feeding the flock is! God is responsible for church growth. In my opinion, every attempt to make a church grow (I'm speaking numerically) is a work of the flesh. I can't think of a single place in the Scriptures where the leadership is told to increase the number of church members. In the Bible, increase in numbers was always the result of faithfully preaching the gospel and feeding the flock!

Feed the flock the pure milk of the Word and true growth will follow.

I remember hearing Greg Laurie say that he had never consciously done anything to make the church grow. That's an interesting statement considering he pastors a church of over ten thousand people! Martyn Lloyd-Jones was once asked why, in his opinion, were there so few men in the churches? His response was, "because there are so many 'old women' in our pulpits!" Lloyd-Jones was not, of course, speaking literally, nor was he speaking disparagingly of older women. He was referring to those men in pulpits who had given up on the hard work of preaching the Word, and had substituted pleasantries, platitudes, and philosophies in its place. Feed the flock the pure milk of the Word and true growth will follow.

Tending the Flock

Tending the flock refers to pastoral care. It speaks of giving personal attention to individual Christians. It means praying with them, counseling them, comforting them, being a friend to them, and loving them. In our big business culture of the West, pastoral care is almost a lost art. Many church leaders today, rather than spending time with people individually, will have a professional counselor on staff, or will refer people to the local Christian psychologist. This is tantamount to religious malpractice in my opinion! A pastor who neglects the sheep is a hireling, according to Jesus, and not really a true pastor at all.[18]

Some men in church leadership today dislike the title pastor because it doesn't have that ring of importance or authority. They prefer something more sophisticated like doctor. Because many ministries are using a management or corporate model, the senior pastor is more like your typical CEO instead of the servant of all, of whom Jesus spoke.[19] The New Testament is full of examples of how our Lord and His apostles took time to minister to individuals; and we need to follow that model. I remember years ago, I was teaching a weekly Bible study for some teenagers, and on this particular occasion, only one person was going to be able to show up for the study that night. Because I knew that only one person was coming, I decided to cancel the study. As I hung the cancellation notice on the door and began to walk away, the Lord spoke to my heart and said, "I ministered to just one. Won't you?"[20] Needless to say, I took down the notice and had the Bible study.

As a pastor, I enjoy teaching the congregation. There is an element of excitement and gratification as I sense the power of the Holy Spirit and as I interact with the people. We don't always have those kinds of experiences as we meet with people one on one, and therefore, we might want to leave that more personal ministry to others.

Over the years, there were times I thought I

would completely put aside personal counseling and leave that to my assistant pastors, concentrating all my energy on study and sermon preparation. Yet, each time I've attempted to do that, the Lord has clearly stopped me. The Lord has shown me that ministering to people on an individual basis helps me to stay in touch with where people are at and with what they are going through. It is easy for pastors to disconnect from the real world and to get caught up in the world of books. We have to maintain a balance, for if the pastor loses touch with the people, he will no longer be effective in his ministry. You might have beautifully laid out sermons filled with a variety of anecdotes collected from your book of ten thousand sermon illustrations, but to the man out in the real world who is just trying to survive, you can appear as though you're from another planet.

If the pastor loses touch with the people, he will no longer be effective in his ministry.

Stay in touch with people. Be available to the people. Shepherd the flock that is *among* you. I understand that as a ministry grows, the pastor might not be able to give the same amount of individual attention to people as he could when the church was smaller. But, we must never lose that shepherd's heart. We must be among the people and accessible to them.

L. E. Romaine once said, "Pulpit men are easy to find, but to find a man with a shepherd's heart is another story." A true shepherd is one who tends as well as feeds the flock.

Leading the Flock

Leading the flock is a very important aspect of pastoral ministry. It has to do with understanding God's will for a congregation and then taking them in that direction. I believe that God has a special emphasis or direction for each particular fellowship, and God will give the pastor wisdom on how to take the people where He wants them to go. The pastor is in many ways like the captain of a team.

Leading is done most effectively by example.

He's not the only player, or even the most important one, but he's the one who is able to bring all the other players together so that the team functions as it ought to. Leading also means that you're able to recognize God's gifts in the lives of others and help them to use them. Leading is to run with the vision that God has given, and to have others follow.

Perhaps you are lacking vision and wondering how to get it. Pray for it. As we seek the Lord, He will reveal to us where He desires to lead His people.

Leading is done most effectively by example. The best way to encourage holiness in people's lives is to be holy ourselves. The best way to teach people the importance of prayer is to be men of prayer. The most effective way to help people live by faith is to step out in faith. If we want people to reach out to the lost, we must reach out to the lost. The church is crying out for leadership, and by the grace of God we must rise to the occasion. As I look back over the years of ministry, I'm afraid I didn't always lead as well as I should have. I let many opportunities pass by simply because of unbelief. Like Moses, I found myself saying, "I'm not able," or like Jeremiah, "I'm just a child."[21] But God has called us to lead His people and has promised to be with us as we go. Let us go forward, then, following Him who is the Great Shepherd of the sheep.[22]

chapter 3

STUDY TO SHOW
YOURSELF APPROVED

Study to shew thyself approved unto God, a workman that [need] not to be ashamed, rightly dividing the word of truth.

—2 Timothy 2:15 KJV

Teaching is a gift that must be cultivated and developed. Unlike prophecy, which is a spontaneous flow of the Spirit, teaching is more dependent on the teacher's education and preparation. Teaching is certainly a spiritual gift, but it involves our natural powers as well—the powers of thought and speech.

Since this is so, we need to do as much as possible to develop these gifts. We cannot expect God to do His part if we're not willing to do our part. If I am going to rightly divide the Word of truth, then I have to study the Word. Before one can be a teacher, one must be taught.

Students have many avenues of learning from which to choose. If we understand that God's means of educating us is not always along the same lines as other forms of education, then we can be open to a fuller and broader preparation. Those who view a traditional form of education as being sufficient preparation for the ministry have underestimated both the task and the nature of the ministry, in my opinion. Even Paul, the most formally educated of the apostles, asked the rhetorical question, "And who is sufficient for these things?"[23] referring to his calling as a minister of the gospel of Jesus Christ. Obviously, he was acknowledging his own sense of inadequacy.

Before one can be a teacher, one must be taught.

A more traditional form of education, like Bible college or seminary, can certainly be profitable, but is by no means mandatory for all. D. L. Moody was a classic case in point. He was uneducated in the traditional sense, but considering his life from another perspective, he was well educated. He understood people and was a gifted communicator, despite his poor grammar. Moody's study habits were unorthodox. Rather than sit down with books, Moody sat down with people. He gleaned from their lives and experiences, and then incorporated the best of what he had learned into his own life and ministry. Moody is an excellent illustration of how God uses different ways to equip His servants.

If God has indeed called a man, He will equip him for the task. We can trust that He will see to our education and preparation.

Our education, as ministers of the gospel, begins with the Scriptures. We must eat, drink, and breathe the Word of God! It was said of Luther that he shocked all Christendom when he stepped forth as a master of the biblical text. May that be true of us as well! How do we become men of the Word? There's no other *If God has indeed called a man, He will equip him for the task.* way but to immerse ourselves in the Bible, as well as good commentaries and resources that will help us know and understand God's Word better.

We also need to realize that God prepares us through the everyday experiences of life. I have learned so much through over twenty-eight years of marriage and the raising of four children—things that I never could have learned in a classroom or from reading a book. These lessons often find their way into my teaching. My children, and now grandchildren, continue to provide me with some of the greatest sermon illustrations.

I also think of the things I've learned by living with a chronic illness for many years, and how that has often helped me to minister more effectively to those who are sick or suffering. Sometimes it's an illustration from my own struggles that God uses to really bless and give hope to others. Illustrations play an important role in communicating God's Word to people. C. H. Spurgeon said, "A sermon without illustrations is like a room without windows."[24] How true that is. Spurgeon himself was a master illustrator; and as you read him, it becomes clear that he was a man with a great knowledge of and love for life itself, nature, history, science, art, etc. There is much to be learned in the classroom of life, so don't get frustrated if it's intruding into your study time. Instead, look for those lessons from life that the Spirit will use to help you as you teach His people His Word.

chapter 4

EXCELLENCE IN MINISTRY

See that you make all things according to the pattern shown you ...

—Hebrews 8:5

The ministry has two sides to it—the divine and the human. Oftentimes, we put so much emphasis on the divine side that we overlook the human element. In doing so, we fail to take into consideration the practical aspects of the ministry. Many times, the ministry suffers and falls short of what God intends it to be because we've neglected this area of need. In this final chapter, I want to focus on the practical or human side of the ministry. Over the years, I've used a few different titles to express the essence of what I'm seeking to communicate when teaching on this subject; titles like: "Doing Ministry Right" and

"Practical Steps to Help Your Church Grow." But I've settled on the title, "Excellence in Ministry," for that seems to express the point more clearly. Let me begin with the pastor.

Intellectual Preparation

The pastor needs to be prepared intellectually. As a forewarning, some of what I am about to say might make you a bit uncomfortable, but please hear me out. When I say intellectually, I mean that we are to make sure we have studied hard, done our homework, and have our facts straight. In referring to historical events, incorporating illustrations, quoting people or statistics, or laying out doctrinal and theological propositions, we need to be accurate. Mistakes are inevitable; we all make them, but we need to learn from our mistakes and try to avoid repeating them. We all, at times, will get things wrong; it is continually doing things incorrectly that we need to avoid. Do not be lazy and just depend on others to do all the work for you; do your own research (in other words, don't just listen to someone else's sermon and get up and repeat it). Know the facts; know what you believe and why you believe it so you can communicate the truth to others with confidence and conviction.

Speech

Another aspect of this is our ability to speak correctly. We want to reach as many people as possible, so we need to speak in a way that enhances that possibility. Can God use a person with a limited vocabulary and bad grammar? Of course He can, and He has. Many of us were in that category at one time. But He can and has used many with a strong vocabulary and good grammar. Many of the great preachers of the past, men whom so many of us look up to, were men who cultivated their powers of speech. Just read C. H. Spurgeon, F. B. Meyer, G. Campbell Morgan, or Martyn Lloyd-Jones, and you will see what I'm saying.

Words are the tools of our trade, and if we are short on words, we will perhaps limit our possibilities for effectiveness. Don't despair if you have a limited vocabulary, but work on developing a stronger one for God's glory. The more you read, use a dictionary, and listen to good speakers, the more your vocabulary will improve.

Many of the great preachers of the past were men who cultivated their powers of speech.

Some might be tempted to just dismiss all of this talk about vocabulary and grammar as petty and unspiritual. I know I've been tempted to do that myself. But God uses these things to help develop us. Spurgeon told his students that the person who helped him immensely with his preaching ministry was the person who every week found some fault in something that he had said. When he first began to receive little notes from this person, he was greatly annoyed, as all of us would be. But as time went on, he began to realize that there was something to it; and rather than being annoyed, he found he could actually learn some valuable lessons. He began taking these critiques as God's way of teaching him to be a more effective communicator—a wise way to look at it.

Appearance and Attitude

What about the pastor's appearance? I think pastors ought to do their best to be well groomed when they are in the pulpit. Now that is going to look different from place to place, and you must decide what is appropriate in the place where God has you ministering. However, if you are in a conservative community, and you show up in jeans and a T-shirt, many folks will have a hard time taking you seriously. Because Calvary Chapel had its beginning in *casual* Southern California, many have had to learn that things are quite a bit different in other parts of the country and around the world. You just don't show up in New York City or London, England, in your cargo shorts and flip-flops and expect people to start flocking to your church.

We all have to make adjustments in order to reach as many people as we can; therefore, we must be flexible and broad in our ministry approach.

Being flexible implies the ability to adapt to new surroundings. Some guys are so rigid that they will not bend at all and instead expect everyone to conform to their likes and preferences. This kind of approach will hinder your ability to minister. Remember the Calvary beatitude: Blessed are the flexible. We also need to be broad, not in a theological sense, but in a cultural sense. We need to be able to accommodate people from other backgrounds and cultures. Having grown up in the Southern California surf culture, I had to make some changes when I moved to London to start a church. I had to forever lose the word "dude" and learn to relate to the British people on their level. It was a lesson worth learning, and it is one of the great joys of ministry to be able to join people from different cultures and nations in worshipping and serving Jesus.

Practical Wisdom and Sanctified Common Sense

In order for a church to function properly, there needs to be a certain amount of organization. But I have noticed over the years that pastors will often overlook the practical or human side of the ministry. Let's look at some of these vitally important issues.

Punctuality

Be punctual; people care about their time. Most people don't want to come to a service that starts late and ends late. Now some of you might feel that this type of structure constrains the Holy Spirit, but if the Holy Spirit wants you to go longer, then you will go longer and no one will complain. More often, people, pastors included, ignore punctuality. They overlook its value. I have even heard churches go so far as to coin a new phrase, "Calvary time," meaning ten minutes late. I don't know where they got this, but it was not from Pastor Chuck. Calvary Chapel Costa Mesa has three Sunday morning services: 7:45, 9:30, and 11:15. These are not estimates; there is no ten-minute delay. They start at those times, every service, every Sunday. Chuck has

Be punctual; people care about their time.

a watch that synchronizes with the satellite, and my watch is within ten seconds of his. We stand behind the platform and count down the seconds. Then we walk up to the pulpit right on time. As crazy as this may seem, we have to understand that a person's time is valuable.

This was yet another lesson that I learned the hard way. As a young pastor, I used to start services late. After all, most people came late and I didn't want to start before the people got there. Back then, I didn't realize that I was perpetuating the problem. All of that changed after a kindly older gentleman mildly rebuked me for my lack of punctuality. He told me that he came to church fifteen minutes early and that my starting the service fifteen minutes late left him sitting and waiting for half an hour. I suddenly realized how inconsiderate that was. From that point on, I decided never to start a service late again.

Punctuality extends to both ends of the service. We start on time. We end on time. We have all been to a service that wouldn't end. People are afraid of quenching the Spirit and on it goes. Remember the congregation. Even if you can ramble for two-and-a-half hours, people cannot sit that long and pay attention. I remember sitting through a great Bible study one time that lasted about an hour. Just as we passed the hour mark and had completed the main portion of the chapter, I was completely shocked when the teacher launched into another forty minutes of teaching. At that point, I not only tuned out what the teacher was saying, I forgot all that he had previously said. It was just too much to digest!

Clean, Convenient, and Comfortable

The condition of the facility the church meets in will leave a lasting impression on people. A church overrun with trash and dirt will chase away even the most devoted members. Most people simply will not attend and they certainly will not bring their children to a dirty facility. Thus, we need to make sure the church is tidy. I know this can be difficult, especially when you rent your building and have to work with what someone else leaves you week after week. In fact, when I was in London, we met in a school whose owners took no pride in it whatsoever. In the few years we were there, the condition went from bad to worse. Every week, we found it filthy. So, every week we cleaned it. I would get there, set my Bible on the pulpit, walk out, grab a broom, and sweep up cigarette butts and all the rest of the rubbish that was left over from the week. Even though the facility was someone else's during the week, it was ours on Sundays. We do not always have control over those kinds of things, so we have to do our best with what we have. Keep things tidy and clean, and people will take note.

I mentioned children earlier. Children's ministry is vital to any church. If you neglect to develop a good, strong children's ministry, you will inevitably hinder the growth of the church. Someone asked me a while back what I considered to be the most necessary elements in starting a church. My response: a pastor/teacher/evangelist, a children's minister, and a worship leader. In that order! Give priority to the kids because they are the future.

Give priority to the kids because they are the future.

We need to keep a couple of other things in mind regarding the facility where the church meets. First is location. You've perhaps heard someone say the key to success in retail is: Location, location, location. Well, there is some truth to that with a church as well. Now I know we've all heard of the fellowship that was hidden in some secluded valley, or off in some obscure, inaccessible part of the city and grew to thousands, but we have to realize that these are the exceptions, not the rule. If people can't find you, they're not going to come! When looking for a facility, prayerfully seek a place with easy access. I have pastored churches in three different locations, and each time the Lord put us in highly visible, easily accessible sites. If for some reason the Lord leads you to some obscure location, then know He has a specific purpose in mind.

The final point I would make regarding the facility has to do with a comfortable environment. Comfort, I realize, is a relative concept. A person's comfort zone is to some degree determined by their living environment. However, having said that, we all know what it is like to be too hot or too cold, or for something to be too loud or too quiet. We know when something is convenient or inconvenient. Do your best to make the church a comfortable place for people to come to worship God and to grow in their knowledge of Him.

Worship

Calvary Chapel has always placed a huge emphasis on music in the services. Music is the universal language that crosses all cultural barriers. That is especially true of praise and worship. Since music plays such a large part in our worship services, we ought to do our best to make sure the music is played skillfully and reverently.

When I say skillfully, I don't mean professionally. I mean simply playing the right chords or notes and singing in the proper key. Many unskilled, would-be worship leaders have ended up being more of a hindrance than a help to the worshippers. No doubt, many have had pure hearts, but even that could not overcome the absence of the musical gene.

It is my opinion that it would be wiser to find a person who can lead a few choruses a cappella rather than have a guitarist who has yet to learn the art of tuning, or worse yet, the art of carrying a tune. The worship leader must be skilled.

Reverently means we are conscious of God's presence and are seeking His glory, not our own.

Worship leaders who draw attention to themselves are contradicting the very purpose of their ministry, which is to point people to the Lord. Besides being skillful and reverent, worship music must also be relevant to the culture we are living in and ministering to. The traditional Calvary style of worship is the acoustic guitar, or the "praise band." That works well in many places and among many cultures, but in some places, it is culturally irrelevant.

I remember talking to a friend of mine who happened to be a black pastor of an all-white church. We were discussing how he might reach out and draw in people from the black community. I knew that he had a blonde-haired, surfer-type guy as his worship leader, so my advice to him was to mix things up a bit and adopt a style of worship that those in the black community could relate to. He did, and today he's pastoring a beautifully multi-ethnic congregation.

The church should always be producing new songs that express the faith and experiences of the present generation.

In the Scriptures, the Lord instructs us to sing a new song.[25] If we resist, we will soon lose touch with the current generation and lose sight of the mission of communicating Christ to them in a way they can relate. There are many great hymns, choruses, and songs from the past, but the church should always be producing new hymns, choruses, and songs that express the faith and experiences of the present generation.

Music plays an important role in our worship services, as we've already noted, but we need to be careful not to overemphasize its importance. The preoccupation with having the best musicians, the best sound system, all of the latest in technology, etc., indicates an imbalanced perspective. Gifted vocalists, talented musicians, and good equipment can be a blessing, but they are by no means essential to a God-honoring, God-glorifying worship service. Keep the balance.

Hospitality

Finally, aim to create a loving, friendly, hospitable environment in your church. The worship service is a concerted effort that involves many people serving in many different roles. Seek to match the right person with the area of ministry for which they are best suited. You would obviously want those who are greeting and welcoming people to the church (especially first-time visitors) to be kind, friendly, and helpful. It can be intimidating for a person or family to visit a new church. We should do our best to make them feel welcome. If you have certain policies that might be a bit challenging for newcomers, be flexible. We have had a policy of not allowing children under six into the main service in order to keep the distractions to a minimum and to make sure the kids are ministered to on their level. This has been a hard pill to swallow for some. I believe it's a good policy, but we are flexible, especially with newcomers.

I remember a few times over the years where a family would visit the church for the first time and the well-intended but totally misguided and insensitive ushers would accost them at the entrance and try to force them to take their kids to the children's ministry. The next thing I knew, that precious family, who was looking for a new church home, was on their way out the door, shaking the dust off their feet as they went! On more than one occasion, I've had to pull an usher aside and give him a fresh reminder of the need for grace, mercy, wisdom, and flexibility. This is what I mean by practical wisdom and sanctified common sense. I think if we just used a bit more of both, along with some common courtesy, we would avoid many of the little things that can frustrate the work the Holy Spirit is wanting to do through the church.

With that being said, may God grant us a heart full of love and a head full of wisdom as we serve Him.

appendix a

RECOMMENDED READING

Books are the tools of the trade for the pastor. The commentaries, books, and authors listed have been helpful to me over the years.

1.   **Commentaries** - *Bible Knowledge Commentary* (Walvoord & Zuck); *Believer's Bible Commentary* (MacDonald); *Thru the Bible Commentary* (J. Vernon McGee); *Application Commentary* (Jon Courson); *The Bible Exposition Commentary* (Warren Wiersbe)

2.   **Commentators** - Martyn Lloyd-Jones; H. A. Ironside; William Newell; Donald Barnhouse; Griffith Thomas; G. Campbell Morgan; F. B. Meyer; C. H. Spurgeon; Alexander McClaren; J. C. Ryle; Leon Morris; John MacArthur; John Stott; James Montgomery Boice; R. Kent Hughes; John Phillips; David Guzik

3. **Systematic Theology** - versions by: Thiessen; Chaffer; Berkhof; Grudem

4. **Bibliology** - *A General Introduction to the Bible* (Geisler & Nix); *The Canon of Scripture* (F. F. Bruce); *Nothing But the Truth* (Brian H. Edwards); *Encyclopedia of Bible Difficulties* (Gleason L. Archer); *When Critics Ask* (Geisler & Howe)

5. **Apologetics' Authors** - C. S. Lewis; Francis Schaeffer; Ravi Zacharias; Norman Geisler; J. P. Moreland; Alister McGrath; William Lane Craig; Gene Edward Veith; James Sire; R. C. Sproul; Josh McDowell; Paul Little; Lee Strobel; Gary Habermas; David Nobel; Dinesh D'Souza

6. **Archaeology/Language** - *The Stones Cry Out* (Randall Price); *Archaeology and the Old Testament* (Unger); *IVP Background Bible Commentary: Old Testament;* also *New Testament* (Keener); *Word Meanings in the New Testament* (Earle); *Expository Dictionary of New Testament Words* (W. E. Vine); *Word Studies in the New Testament* (Wuest)

7. **Creation versus Evolution** - *Darwin's Black Box* (Michael Behe); *Darwin on Trial* (Phillip Johnson); *The Long War Against God;* also *The Modern Creation Trilogy* (Henry Morris); *The World That Perished* (Whitcomb); *Man's Origin,*

Man's Destiny (A. E. Wilder-Smith); *Creation and Change* (Douglas F. Kelly)

8. **Cults** - *Kingdom of the Cults* (Walter Martin); *The Challenge of the Cults* (Ron Rhodes); *So What's the Difference?* (Fritz Ridenour)

9. **World Religions** - *A Compact Guide to World Religions* (Halverson); *Handbook of Today's Religions* (McDowell & Stewart); *Answering Islam* (Geisler & Saleeb); *The Cross and the Crescent* (Phil Parshall); *Glad News! God Loves You My Muslim Friend* (Samy Tanagho); *Secrets of the Koran* (Don Richardson); *Roman Catholics and Evangelicals* (Geisler & MacKenzie); *Roman Catholicism* (L. Boettner); *Exploring the World of the Jew* (Phillips); *The Christian and the Pharisee* (Dr. R. T. Kendall & Rabbi David Rosen)

10. **Eschatology** - *The Millennial Kingdom* (Walvoord); *Things to Come* (J. Dwight Pentecost); *Israel in the Spotlight* (Charles Feinberg); *Israel in the Plan of God* (David Baron)

11. **Ministry Helps** - *Preaching and Preachers* (Martyn Lloyd-Jones); *Between Two Worlds* (John Stott); *On Being a Pastor* (Alistair Begg & Derek Prime)

12. **Biographies** - *Moody* (John Pollock); *Spurgeon*

(Arnold Dalimore); *D. Martyn Lloyd-Jones* (Iain Murray); *Charles Wesley* (Arnold Dalimore); *A. B. Simpson* (A. W. Tozer); *H. A. Ironside* (E. Shulyer English); *J. Hudson Taylor* (Roger Steer); *George Müller* (Roger Steer); *George Whitefield* (Arnold Dalimore); *Walking with Giants* (Warren Wiersbe); *That Man Barnhouse* (Margaret N. Barnhouse); *Just as I Am* (Billy Graham); *John Stott* (Timothy Dudly-Smith)

13. **History: Biblical, Church, and Secular** - *Old Testament Bible History; also The Life and Times of Jesus the Messiah* (Alfred Edersheim); *The Life and Epistles of St. Paul* (Conybeare & Howson); *Paul, Apostle of the Heart Set Free* (F. F. Bruce); *A History of Christianity* (Kenneth Scott Latourette); *Church History in Plain Language* (Bruce Shelly); *Christianity's Dangerous Idea* (Alister McGrath); *From Jerusalem to Irian Jaya* (Ruth Tucker); *Let the Nations Be Glad* (John Piper); *Eternity in Their Hearts* (Don Richardson); *A Short History of the World* (J. M. Roberts); *A Study of History* (Arnold Toynbee); *Intellectuals; also Modern Times* (Paul Johnson); *Israel* (Martin Gilbert); *The Fight for Jerusalem; also Hatred's Kingdom* (Dore Gold); *Islam: A Short History* (Karen Armstrong); *Islamic Imperialism: A History* (Efraim Karsh)

appendix b

SERMON OUTLINES

In this appendix, I've included two outlines that will hopefully be helpful in giving an example of what a sermon outline and a Bible study outline look like. The outline from John's gospel is more sermonic, while the outline from Romans is more of a verse-by-verse exposition of the text. In the case of the outline from John 8, you'll notice there is an introduction, followed by a number of points and sub points, and then a conclusion. I would refer to this as an outline for expository preaching. The Romans outline is more of an expositional teaching outline (exposition meaning a commentary on a written text discussing its meaning and implications).

The simplest way for me to differentiate between preaching and teaching is that a sermon is preached and a Bible study is taught. On Sunday mornings, I preach a sermon; on Wednesday evenings, I teach a Bible study. In a sermon, I am primarily exhorting and challenging both believers and unbelievers. In a Bible study, I am primarily instructing believers. There is obviously an overlap in both cases. In other words, there's an instructional element in the sermon, and there's an element of application and exhortation in the Bible study.

THE WAY TO FREEDOM

John 8:31–36

Introduction: Perhaps the greatest ideal of the twenty-first century is that of freedom. Monarchy, oligarchy, or anything even remotely resembling totalitarianism is out and democracy is in—the current definition of democracy being that of total autonomy: the absolute freedom to do whatever one desires. My intention here is not to discuss which system is right or wrong, but to point out how highly valued freedom is in the thinking of most people today. Jesus placed a high value on freedom, not freedom in a political sense, not even freedom in a personal sense, but freedom in a spiritual sense. Freedom from sin! Sin is man's greatest oppressor, and Jesus Christ came to break the tyranny of sin over people's lives. Here in our text Jesus tells us practically how that happens. There is a promise and there is a condition. Let's look first at the promise, then we will look at the condition.

I. **The Promise** - twofold

    A. You shall know the truth.

What a wonderful promise. The real meaning and purpose of life cannot be known or attained apart from the knowledge of the truth. To what truth is Jesus referring?

    1. Truth about God—His existence, His plan, His love, His grace, His power.

    2. Truth about man—His origin, his plight, his destiny.

B. The truth shall make you free.

The freedom Jesus is talking about here is freedom from the bondage of sin.

    1. Every human being is born a slave of sin.

You might say, wait a minute, that's a bit extreme I was never a slave of sin. I wasn't a drug addict, an alcoholic, a violent person, a kleptomaniac, a habitual liar, or a sexual pervert. That might be true, but Jesus said right here, "He that commits sin is a slave of sin." In the ancient world not every slave appeared to be a slave. Some slaves enjoyed a tremendous amount of freedom, power, and prestige, while others were in abject slavery. So it is with slavery to sin. Not everyone appears to be in bondage to sin, but we all are.

2. Jesus is promising deliverance from the bondage of sin. It is the promise of an ongoing process of liberation by which we're being continually delivered from the power of sin. Sin is powerful, perhaps the greatest power in the universe, apart from God. Sin is also tenacious—it doesn't want to let go of us. Sin will fight to hang on to the bitter end and that's why we must actively pursue total emancipation from its hold on our lives.

3. This is where the condition of the promise of freedom comes into the picture.

II. The Condition

A. Disciple - a follower, a totally devoted follower. It's the disciples of Jesus who are set free from the power of sin.

B. Abide - *Syn.* reside, remain, continue, live in.

C. The Word - abide implies both meditation and obedience.

1. Meditate - Josh. 1:8; Ps. 1; Col. 3:16

   a. Study the Word.

    b. Personally meditate on the Word.

In a recent interview, 88-year-old Billy Graham said this: "Almost since the night I accepted Christ into my life as a teenager, I have tried to set aside time each morning to be alone with God. This time includes prayer, reading the Bible, and meditating on its meaning. Nothing has been more important to my spiritual life."

    c. Obey the Word - doers of Word not hearers only.

Close: Are you free from the bondage of sin? If so, good! That means you're abiding in His Word. Are you bound up in sin? Do you find yourself doing things you know you shouldn't do, even doing things you don't want to do? If so, I can tell you why. You're not abiding in His Word. Maybe you're saying, "I don't think that's really the answer to my problem. I don't see how the Word can really help me; I think my problems are bigger than that." Listen, God spoke the universe into existence. He said, let there be light and there was light. He said, let the waters be gathered together and the dry land appear and it was so. He said, let the waters abound with living creatures and the earth bring forth the living creature according to its kind and it was so. He said to the lame man, rise up and walk. He said to the blind man, receive your sight. He said to the dead man, arise. He says to you today, abide in My Word and you shall know the truth and the truth shall make you free.

> I knew a young man named Charlie,
> He went and lost his way
> Now he's in prison, cold prison
> No chance to escape
> They gave him new clothes and a Bible, and the Word he did read
> Now the four walls can't keep him 'cause Charlie is free.
>
> Jonny Lang[26]

Freedom is indeed a glorious ideal, but true freedom can only come through Christ.

Therefore, if the Son makes you free, you shall be free indeed.

ROMANS

Chapter 1:1

Introduction: Although Romans was not the first epistle written by the apostle Paul, it has been placed first in our New Testament; and rightfully so, for it is first in importance.

Romans, of all Paul's letters, comes nearest to being a theological treatise. In almost all his other letters he is dealing with some immediate trouble, some pressing situation, some current error, or some threatening danger that was menacing the church to which he was writing. Romans is the nearest approach to a systematic exposition of Paul's own theological position independent of any immediate set of circumstances.

Romans is the epistle in which we are face to face with all the foundational truths of the Scripture.

Dr. Lloyd-Jones said: " There is a sense in which we can say quite truthfully that the Epistle to the Romans has, possibly, played a more important and more crucial part in the history of the church than any other single book in the whole of the Bible."

Romans has indeed been used by God in an exceptional manner.

    a.   Augustine AD 387

    b.   Luther AD 1517

    c.   Wesley AD 1738

    d.   Chuck Smith AD 1953

The epistle begins with the author introducing himself.

I. Paul.

Who was this man Paul? What was his background? What qualified him to write more of the New Testament than any other author?

These important questions should not be overlooked. Many Bible teachers make a mistake when they rush too quickly past the introductory verses of these Epistles. As you'll see, there's much here for the Christian to feed on.

    A.   Paul's background - "I am indeed a Jew, born in Tarsus of Cilicia, but brought up in this city at the feet of Gamaliel, taught according to the strictness of our fathers' law, and was zealous toward God ..." (Acts 22:3).

1. Zealous - "Indeed, I myself thought I must do many things contrary to the name of Jesus of Nazareth. This I also did in Jerusalem, and many of the saints I shut up in prison, having received authority from the chief priests; and when they were put to death, I cast my vote against them. And I punished them often in every synagogue and compelled them to blaspheme; and being exceedingly enraged against them, I persecuted them even to foreign cities" (Acts 26:9–11).

2. Conversion - Road to Damascus

B. Paul was uniquely equipped to be the apostle to the Gentiles.

1. As a Jew and a Pharisee, he would be able to successfully defend the new faith from Judaism's attempt to destroy it.

2. Born in Tarsus, he understood Greek culture, which would bring some advantage in his ministry to the Gentiles.

3. Being a Roman citizen, he would enjoy many privileges that would enhance his ability to proclaim the gospel.

C. God often takes our background and the things that we might consider as purely natural and uses them for His glory.

II. A Bondservant of Jesus Christ.

A. One who serves another willingly and out of love.

B. One whose will is swallowed up in the will of another.

III. An Apostle. This is what qualified Paul to write much of the New Testament.

A. Definition - An apostle is one chosen and sent with a special mission as the fully authorized representative of the sender.

B. The Scriptures tell us five things about apostles.

1. They were appointed by the Lord Himself.

"And He went up on the mountain and called to Him those He Himself wanted. And they came to Him. Then He appointed twelve, that they might be with Him and that He might send them out to preach, and to have power to heal sicknesses and to cast out demons."

Mark 3:13–15

2.   They had to have seen the risen Lord.

And in those days Peter stood up in the midst of the disciples (altogether the number of names was about a hundred and twenty), and said, "... of these men who have accompanied us all the time that the Lord Jesus went in and out among us, beginning from the baptism of John to that day when He was taken up from us, one of these must become a witness with us of His resurrection."

Acts 1:15, 21–22

Am I not an apostle? Am I not free? Have I not seen Jesus Christ our Lord? Are you not my work in the Lord?

1 Corinthians 9:1

3.   They had authority to perform miracles.

Truly the signs of an apostle were accomplished among you with all perseverance, in signs and wonders and mighty deeds.

2 Corinthians 12:12

4.   They had power to impart the gifts of the Holy Spirit.

Therefore I remind you to stir up the gift of God which is in you through the laying on of my hands.

2 Timothy 1:6

5. They were commissioned to write the Scriptures.

Therefore, beloved, looking forward to these things, be diligent to be found by Him in peace, without spot and blameless; and consider that the longsuffering of our Lord is salvation—as also our beloved brother Paul, according to the wisdom given to him, has written to you, as also in all his epistles, speaking in them of these things, in which are some things hard to understand, which untaught and unstable people twist to their own destruction, as they do also the rest of the Scriptures.

2 Peter 3:14–16

C. Are there apostles today? No and Yes.

Close: Paul said he was **called** to be an apostle.

a. Paul did not think of life in terms of what he wanted to do, but in terms of what God meant him to do.

b. Like Paul, each of us has a call upon our lives. We are called first to salvation, then to sanctification, and then to service. Have you heeded that call?

NOTES

1   Spurgeon, C. H. The Spurgeon Archive, "The Sound in the Mulberry Trees," http://www.spurgeon.org/sermons/0147.htm.

2   John 21:17

3   1 Peter 5:2

4   1 Timothy 4:13

5   2 Corinthians 2:16

6   John 15:5

7   Romans 7:18

8   2 Timothy 1:9

9   1 Peter 1:16; also see Leviticus 11:44

10   Acts 11

11   Jeremiah 23:1–2; Ezekiel 34

12   2 Peter 2

13   Jeremiah 23:4

14   Acts 20:27

15   1 Timothy 4:13

16   2 Timothy 4:2

17   Acts 5:42

18   John 10:12–13

19   Mark 9:35

20   John 4:1–42

21   Exodus 3:11; see Jeremiah 1:6

22   Hebrews 13:20

23   2 Corinthians 2:16

24   Spurgeon, C. H. The Spurgeon Archive, "Sermons in Candles," http://www.spurgeon.org/misc/candles.htm.

25   Psalm 33:3

26   Lang, Jonny (September 2006). "Turn Around." Turn Around: CD, Monrovia, CA: A&M Records.

CONTACT INFORMATION

If you have questions or would like more information regarding Pastor Brian's ministry, please call the following numbers:

In the US:

714-979-4422

In the UK:

+44 (0)20 8466 5365

You may also go to the following Web site for information:

www.backtobasicsradio.com

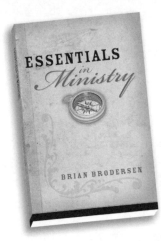

ESSENTIALS IN MINISTRY
By Brian Brodersen

978-1-59751-033-2

Essentials in Ministry, companion to *Excellence in Ministry*, takes a much-needed look at the core areas of ministry and includes a practical and peaceful answer to the Emergent and Church Growth debates. You will also find the answers to such questions as: "What are the essential components of ministry?" and "What is the church supposed to look like today?"

Retail orders, contact:
The Word For Today
www.twft.com
800-272-9673

Wholesale orders, contact:
Calvary Distribution
www.calvaryd.org
800-444-7664